THE
1980s

Richard Tames

Franklin Watts

New York · London · Toronto · Sydney

© 1990 Franklin Watts

Franklin Watts Inc.
387 Park Avenue South
New York, NY 10016

Design: K and Co
Editor: Hazel Poole
Picture Research: Sarah Ridley

Printed in Belgium

Library of Congress Cataloging-in-Publication Data

Tames, Richard.
    The 1980s/Richard Tames.
       p. cm. — (Picture history of the 20th century)
    Summary: Text and pictures highlight the main events of the 1980s.
    ISBN 0-531-14079-2
    1. History, Modern—1945- —Pictorial works—Juvenile literature.
    [1. History, Modern—1945-] I. Title. II. Series.
    D1051.T35 1990
    909.82—dc20
    90-11999 CIP AC

Photographs: Amstrad 26(T), 36(B); Laura Ashley Ltd 38(BL), 38(BR); AP/Wide World Photos 25(CR), 28(B), 29(BR), 34(BL); Cocoa Cola Foods 39(BL); courtesy of Department of Health and Social Security 27(B); Exall Show Ltd 34(TL); courtesy of The Green Party 24(T); Hong Kong Tourist Association 23(BL), 23(BR); Bobbie Kingsley 37(BL); Kobal Collection 32(T), 32(BR), 33(C), Kobal Collection/Lucasfilm Ltd 33(BL), 33(BR); with thanks to Mercury Car Phones 37(TR); National Film Archive/courtesy of Curzon Film Distributors 33(T); Photo Researchers Inc 29(BL); Popper 6(T), 6(BL), 7(BL), 8(B), 9(TR), 10(TR), 13(TL), 14(T), 16(BOTH), 17(T), 17(BR), 18(B), 19(B), 20 (BOTH), 22(T), 25(TL), 27(T), 31(BR), 32(BL), 35(B), 36(T), 38(T), 40(T), 40(BR), 41(BL), 42(B), 44(ALL), 45(ALL); Really Useful Theatre Company/Polydor 34(TR); Reuters/Bettman 30(B), 39(BR); Rex Features 17(BL), 23(TL), 35(BL); Frank Spooner Pictures Ltd 6(BR), 7(T), 7(BR), 8(T), 9(TL), 9(B), 10(BL), 10(BR), 11(ALL), 12(BOTH), 13(TR), 13(B), 14(B), 15(ALL), 17(CR), 18(T), 19(TL), 19(TR), 21(ALL), 22(B), 23(CR), 25(BL), 27(C), 28(T), 30(T), 31(TR), 31(CL), 35(T), 35(CR), 37(TL), 39(T), 40(BL), 41(T), 41(BR), 42(T), 43(T), 43(BR); TRH Pictures 26 (BL), TRH/NASA 43(BL), TRH/Sony 34 (BR); UPI/Bettmann 29(T), 31(TL); George Whiteley (PRI) 37(BR); Woods Hole Oceanographic Institute 26(BR); ZEFA 24(B).

cover: Frank Spooner Pictures Ltd/Gamma
frontispiece: TRH Pictures

Contents

Introduction

In 1989, a State Department researcher from the United States, Francis Fukuyama, won brief notoriety by proclaiming "the end of history" which, on close examination, turned out to be the triumph of liberal democracy and free enterprise in areas where it might least be expected to happen – in the communist regimes of Eastern Europe. Even South Africa appeared to be moving seriously toward a more open political system. Chile and Pakistan, too, had voted to return to democracy. If skeptics denied that this constituted the end of history and could find little cause for optimism in many other parts of the world, they had to admit that, as far as the Western powers were concerned, the mood of world politics was very different from that at the beginning of the decade.

Nineteen eighty had seen the Soviet invasion of Afghanistan and the outbreak of war between Iran and Iraq. In the years following, President Ronald Reagan had denounced the Soviet Union as an "evil empire" and Margaret Thatcher, reveling in the title of "Iron Lady," had rejoiced at Britain's victory over Argentina in the South Atlantic.

By the end of the decade, the United States and the Soviet Union had signed a breakthrough agreement on nuclear missile reduction and the communist dictatorships of eastern Europe had been toppled.

Technologically speaking, it was the decade of chips with everything as new information-processing technologies made their impact felt from the high-tech research laboratory to the supermarket checkout. The world was fast becoming a global village. Millions of television visitors instantaneously witnessing international events began to realize that environmental and political problems on any one continent could affect communities everywhere on earth.

Reagan's America

As Americans celebrated the bicentennial of their Constitution, Ronald Reagan was serving his second term as president. He had already managed to reduce government spending on social programs, income taxes, and business regulations in order to strengthen the private sector of the economy – the "Reagan Revolution." Despite the potentially damaging Iran-Contra scandal, the president left the White House as popular as when he first entered it.

Critics of the Reagan administration noted major failures of policy with the rise of the drug menace, falling standards in education, the loss of international competitiveness and the transformation of the United States from the world's greatest creditor to the world's greatest debtor.

Ronald Reagan retired in 1989 with the satisfaction of seeing his vice-president, George Bush, replace him as his chosen successor.

◁ Oliver North arranged arms sales to Iran hoping to free hostages, and then transferred the funds to Nicaraguan Contras.

△ "The Great Communicator," an official portrait. The smile was characteristic of his light-hearted style.

△ The First Lady's elegance attracted criticism as well as praise. So did her protectiveness.

◁ The drug menace became America's main problem, with ramifications that were legal, medical, economic, political and even diplomatic as the government grappled with both the demand and the supply side of the issue.

▽ The troubled face of Jimmy Carter. Hardworking and idealistic, he ended his presidency in frustration · and humiliating failure when his attempts to resolve the Iranian hostage crisis by means of a daring rescue bid went disastrously wrong.

◁ Bush's eight-year apprenticeship as vice-president gave America's allies confidence in the continuity of U.S. policy abroad as well as at home.

A Russian Revolution

The long era of Soviet stagnation under the rule of Leonid Brezhnev saw little sign of change under his short-lived successors – Yuri Andropov and Konstantin Chernenko. Mikhail Gorbachev, however, determined to tackle his country's problems with the twin weapons of *glasnost* (openness) and *perestroika* (restructuring). His frank acknowledgment of the failures of communism revealed massive inefficiency in the economy and gross mismanagement of public finances and stirred up nationalist aspirations from the Baltic to the Caucasus which threatened to run out of control. Russia's Warsaw Pact allies were faced with the choice of following his example or trying to protect their countries from its effects.

▽ Gorbachev and Raisa go "walkabout" in Tallinn, the capital of Estonia. His goal to improve Soviet consumer goods was frustrated by long-standing economic inefficiency.

▷ Leonid Brezhnev's 17-year rule was attacked by reformers as an era in which bureacratic incompetence stifled initiative but allowed corruption to flourish unchecked.

△ Gorbachev's concern to end superpower confrontation was driven by the need to cut back on arms spending.

△ The Soviet withdrawal from Afghanistan in 1988 ended a 10-year war which had lost them 10,000 men. Surprisingly, the pro-Marxist Afghan government did not fall to the divided Mujahedin guerillas.

◁ A nationalist demonstration in Baku, capital of Azerbaijan, which disputed control of the Armenian territory Nagorny Karabakh. In the Baltic states, nationalists aspired to complete independence

Europe

During the 1980s, the European Economic Community became much more of a community as stronger ties of trade and tourism pulled its peoples closer together and politicians and officials found common causes in dealing with the rest of the world.

"The Nine" became "The Twelve" with the admission to membership of Spain, Portugal, and Greece, creating the world's largest potential market – 300,000,000 consumers.

The history of Eastern Europe was far more dramatic. Poland led the way, moving from the repression of martial law to the installation of the Warsaw Pact's first non-Communist government in 40 years. Hungary embraced market economics eagerly as its Communist party declared itself not Communist at all, but Socialist. East Germany followed suit, raising the possibility of reunifying Germany as a single state.

Czechoslovakia and Bulgaria surprised themselves with similar peaceful revolutions, which revealed legacies of corruption as well as incompetence. Less happy was the re-emergence of crude ethnic rivalries in Yugoslavia. Both East and West Europeans faced the need to find a way to what Gorbachev had called a "common European home."

▽ On July 21, 1987, work began on the Channel Tunnel, linking Britain and France by rail. The first phase of the three-tunnel plan was due for completion in 1993.

▷ On February 23, 1981, Lt. Col. Tejero of the Spanish civil guard attempted a coup by seizing members of the Cortes. King Juan Carlos's personal intervention saved the day.

(Below right) Lech Walesa, leader of Poland's free trade union, Solidarity, campaigns in his native village of Plock.

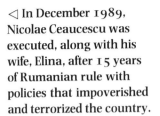

◁ In December 1989,
Nicolae Ceaucescu was
executed, along with his
wife, Elina, after 15 years
of Rumanian rule with
policies that impoverished
and terrorized the country.

△ In November 1989, the
Berlin Wall, erected in
1961 as the most powerful
symbol of the Cold War
and a divided Europe, was
at last demolished.

◁ Rejoicing East Berliners
flood to the West to see the
sights and to reclaim their
most basic freedom, that of
movement. Most,
however, were still content
to go home the same night.

The Middle East: Islam Awakes

Western journalists throughout the decade wrote of a worldwide "Islamic revival." Those who knew better realized that it had never lost its hold on ordinary Muslims who now struggled to redefine their hopes for the future and to challenge the dominance of the non-Muslim West.

Ayatollah Khomeini, having led a broad coalition to overthrow the westernizing Shah of Iran in 1979, then focused the momentum of revolution into the creation of an "Islamic Republic" which horrified Western observers with its violation of human rights, but could still command sufficient loyalty to withstand a crippling war with neighboring Iraq.

Iran's example inspired both the underdog Shiites in war-torn Lebanon and the Palestinians living under Israeli occupation. In Afghanistan, Islam also provided a rallying cry for the politically-fragmented guerilla resistance to a Soviet-backed Marxist regime. Colonel Khadaffi's Libya went its own way while its neighbors, meanwhile, kept a wary eye on political dissent disguised as piety.

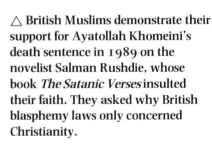

△ British Muslims demonstrate their support for Ayatollah Khomeini's death sentence in 1989 on the novelist Salman Rushdie, whose book *The Satanic Verses* insulted their faith. They asked why British blasphemy laws only concerned Christianity.

◁ The "money rush" of the 1970s was over but the citizens of oil-rich Saudi Arabia could now enjoy the transformations it had brought about. The challenge for the 1980s was to develop the people's own skills and education.

△ In October 1981, Egyptian President Anwar Sadat was assassinated as he reviewed the annual parade to mark the 1973 Yom Kippur war against Israel. His assassins were Muslim extremists opposed to his moderate foreign policy.

△ Ayatollah Khomeini, exiled from 1963 to 1979 for persistent criticism of the Shah, receives a rapturous welcome home as he assumes the spiritual leadership of the anti-Western "Islamic Revolution."

▷ The Iran-Iraq war ended in a ceasefire in July 1988. After eight years of fighting and a million deaths, the outcome was a stalemate despite Iraq's willingness to resort to rockets and chemical weapons.

Latin America

To the Western powers, Latin America ceased to be a picturesque irrelevance in the 1980s. Argentina made good her long-standing claim to the Malvinas/Falklands by an invasion which delighted her people and stunned the British but ended in defeat and humiliation.

In the United States, Congressional politics focused on the attempts of President Reagan to aid the rebel "Contras" against the left-wing Sandinista government of Nicaragua and the concern of the Democrats to stop him. But America and its allies soon began to realize the extent of their involvement in Latin America through the three interlinked issues of drugs, debts, and development. Columbia, Bolivia, and Panama emerged as key links in a chain of supply for the drug pushers whose activities ravaged entire American communities.

Development of rain forest areas, however, threatened local species and gave great concern, worldwide, over environmental damage.

△ President Leopoldo Galtieri assures the Argentine people of continuing victory after the first day's fighting against British forces during the Falklands War. His mishandling of the conflict cost him his office, his rank, and his personal freedom.

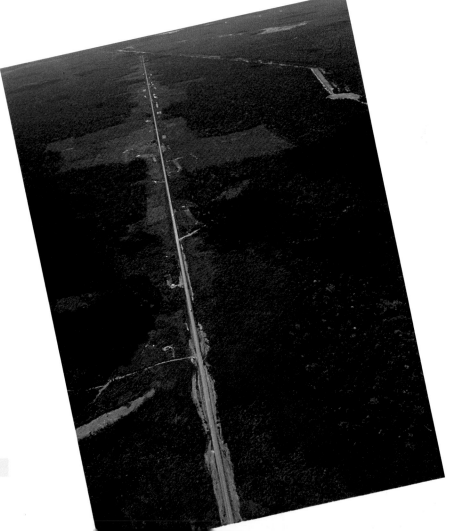

◁ A new road slices through Amazonian rain forest. Brazil's efforts to develop its huge interior and relieve its crowded coastline not only destroyed vast areas of vegetation but also disrupted the lives of isolated tribal peoples.

▷ General Augusto Pinochet imposed more than a decade of authoritarian rule and economic restraint on Chile, but then allowed a referendum that set the country back on the path to democratic government.

▽ Panama's General Manuel Noriega used a combination of pseudo-patriotic gestures and thuggish repression to hang on to power until the American invasion of Christmas 1989 installed a democratic government whose election the dictator had cancelled. Noriega was later deported to the United States to face drug-trafficking charges.

▽ Contra rebels inside Nicaragua. Reagan's support for what he saw as pro-democratic forces brought fierce Congressional criticism.

Africa: the Fight for Freedom

In the 1980s, the West saw Africa as a continent of diminished hopes. The white people of Southern Rhodesia had at last accepted black majority rule in an independent Zimbabwe after a long armed conflict. But the ferocious struggles for power in countries such as Mozambique, Chad, and Uganda brought the problems of arms spending, refugees, and insecurity. Dramatic television reports of the impact of the drought in Ethiopia and the Sudan horrified Western observers and prompted an unprecedented series of fund-raising efforts through music and sport to help the suffering.

South Africa, the continent's only industrialized power, continued to stumble toward a new political balance between a white community split into hard-line and reformist groups and an ever-growing, self-confident black majority, encouraged by international pressures for an end to apartheid.

The cultural outlook was much brighter as African athletes performed brilliantly at world level and African musicians exerted a growing influence on global tastes. But the threat of a catastrophic AIDS epidemic overshadowed the prospects for the 1990s.

△ An Ethiopian child at a relief camp on the Sudanese-Ethiopian border. Built for 5,000 refugees, it actually sheltered over 22,000. The child died later on the same day that this photograph was taken.

◁ A family retrieves what they can from the wreckage of their home destroyed by floods which inundated Khartoum, the capital of the Sudan, in August 1988. In the south, the country was plagued by a long-running civil war.

▽ The first prime minister of independent Zimbabwe, Robert Mugabe. Ten years later, he was still firmly in power in a one-party state.

△ Anti-apartheid campaigner Bishop Desmond Tutu negotiates unsuccessfully with South African forces to allow mourners to accompany a funeral procession.

▽ Youssou N'Dour – singer, composer, drummer, and superstar of African music. The son of Senegalese musicians, he moved to Paris with his band, Super Etoile.

▽ Wole Soyinka (center), a Nigerian novelist who won the Nobel prize for literature in 1986.

South Asia

Disaster and conflicts grabbed the headlines about Southern Asia, hiding the fact that progress was being made in raising living standards. However, violence between different religious communities was a persistent problem.

India, the world's largest democracy, remained under the domination of the Gandhi family until Rajiv Gandhi lost the election of 1989 following allegations of corruption.

The death of President Zia-ul-Haq was followed by elections which made Benazir Bhutto prime minister of Pakistan and the Muslim world's first woman leader. Sri Lanka, torn by the efforts of its Tamil minority to establish an independent homeland, accepted an Indian peace-keeping force. This, however, made things worse and India was asked to withdraw. In Bangladesh, meanwhile, General Hossain Ershad came to power in 1982, bringing with him a period of stability.

△ Indira Gandhi, daughter of India's founder, Nehru, served as Prime Minister in 1966–67 and 1980–84. Assassinated in 1984 by her own Sikh bodyguards in revenge for the assault on the Golden Temple at Amritsar, she was succeeded by her son, Rajiv.

◁ In December 1984 a poison-gas leak from an American-owned pesticide plant at Bhopal, India, killed 2,000 people and injured nearly 200,000 more in the world's worst chemical disaster. It took five years to reach a compensation agreement for the victims.

△ Oxford-educated Benazir Bhutto votes in the 1988 election and follows her father, who was executed in 1979, as prime minister of Pakistan.

△ The revolt of the Tamil guerillas won them more political freedom in East and North Sri Lanka, but angered the majority Sinhalese community.

▷ Cycle rickshaws battle with the 1988 monsoon which affected two-thirds of the people of Bangladesh. International funding for flood control was pledged in 1989.

19

Southeast Asia

The Association of South East Asian Nations (ASEAN) continued to develop as a successful organization for regional cooperation. United by anxiety about Vietnam's military power, the six states enjoyed a decade of economic success marked by increasing progress in industrialization and tourism. This lessened their dependence on the exploitation of raw materials, which was seen as a timely development in the light of growing concerns for the environment and especially for the region's threatened rain forests.

Popular discontent ended over 20 years of Marcos rule in the Philippines, but similar efforts in Burma were violently suppressed as the army-backed Burma Socialist Program Party finally gave way to direct army rule. Cambodia benefited from a breathing space for recovery under 10 years of Vietnamese occupation after the traumas of Pol Pot's Khmer Rouge genocide, but steeled itself against his return when the Vietnamese withdrew in 1989. Within Vietnam itself, the displacement of the guerilla leadership in 1986 showed a willingness to try new ways of restoring the country's war-shattered economy.

△ "People Power" – Corazon (Cory) Aquino, widow of murdered Filipino opposition leader Benigno Aquino, inherited his role as critic of the corrupt and oppressive Marcos regime.

◁ Ferdinand and Imelda Marcos serenade supporters, but for them the song had ended. He died in 1989 and she was exiled.

◁ Fit for a king – the mosque (foreground) and palace (background) built for the sultan of oil-rich Brunei, the richest man in the world. Manpower shortage limited the ability of his mini-state to develop independently.

▷ Refugees at a camp on the border of Thailand and Kampuchea – a tragic reminder of the political tensions threatening the region's growing economic success.

◁ An assembly line at the Honda factory in Bangkok. Japanese industrial investment was drawn into ASEAN by cheaper labor and raw material costs and access to dynamic expanding markets.

East Asia

Japan's status as an economic superpower was confirmed in the eighties by its upward revaluation of the yen, its continuing massive trade surpluses and its spectacular display of overseas investments.

Accepting that wealth brought wider responsibilities, Japan also became the world's largest donor of foreign aid. Domestically, it was much embarrassed by scandals concerning the ruling Liberal Democratic Party's "money politics" and in 1989, the country had no less than three prime ministers.

The neighboring countries of Hong Kong, Singapore, Taiwan, and South Korea emerged as major traders in their own right, abandoning cheap manufactures in favor of high-tech products.

China, likewise, pursued economic modernization with some success but found it impossible to combine this with greater political freedom for its people. Consequently, China ended the decade internationally condemned for its internal repression.

△ Deng Xiao ping, the great political survivor and architect of China's economic liberalization, used power fiercely, despite his increasing frailty.

◁ The aftermath of the mass student sit-in at Beijing's Tiananmen Square in June 1989. Protesters were literally crushed by the tanks of the "People's Army."

◁ Japan's new emperor, Akihito, mourns the death of his father, Hirohito. Representatives of a record number of governments attended the funeral.

▽ The Seoul Olympic Games of 1988 were a brilliant organizational success. South Korea's progress toward democracy was also something to shout about.

◁ The Hong Kong and Shanghai Bank in Hong Kong, the most expensive building in Asia, celebrated the colony's prosperity. But Chinese rule after 1997 threatened uncertainty.

Going Green

At the beginning of the 1980s, few people outside scientific circles were familiar with the terms *ecology, acid rain* or *ozone layer*. By the end of the decade, they had become a part of everyday language. Increasing action to control the human impact on the natural world reflected both a wider popular awareness and systematic government action.

The European Economic Community set standards for clean air, water, and beaches against which member states should measure their own performance. The United Nations promoted international agreements to protect the Antarctic and marine life. The U.S. Environmental Protection Agency virtually banned all use of leaded gasoline in automobiles. The anxieties of an increasingly aware public led governments to impose stricter controls on the use of pesticides, the disposal of hazardous wastes and the management of nuclear and chemical installations.

Commercial companies and political parties also responded to the surge of concern.

**The earth can't vote
You can, vote Green**

△ An election poster for a European Green Party warns that the planet is in danger and that a new voice is needed for the sake of our common future.

RAINBOW WARRIOR

◁ In 1985, the Greenpeace ship *Rainbow Warrior* was blown up in New Zealand on the eve of a protest against French nuclear tests in the Pacific. French secret agents were later found guilty.

◁ In 1986, the Chernobyl power plant near Kiev, capital of the Ukraine, released deadly radiation causing the evacuation of 135,000 people from the surrounding area and contaminating livestock as far away as Wales. Estimates of risks of cancer deaths range from 8,000 upwards.

△ On February 22, 1983, the Federal Government offered to relocate residents of Times Beach, Missouri, after large amounts of the cancer-causing chemical dioxin were discovered in the soil.

◁ President Arap Moi of Kenya burns millions of pounds worth of elephant tusks – a dramatic gesture of determination to stamp out the illegal ivory trade.

25

Science and Medicine

In the 1980s, the microchip and the laser moved out of the research laboratory and into the factory, the office and the home. Computers were reduced to desk top dimensions and used for the design and production of goods as well as the processing of information about them. Operations such as heart and lung transplants became almost a matter of routine. Advances in the field of super conductors offered promises of cheaper, more efficient transmission of electricity in the future. The *Challenger* disaster and the onset of AIDS, however, were sharp reminders that both science and medicine had limits to their powers.

The tendency of previous decades was further exaggerated as consumers and policy-makers accepted and relied upon technological marvels whose workings they could scarcely grasp. The general public were also asked to pass judgment on topics as wide-ranging as the ethics of embryo research and the desirability of irradiating everyday foodstuffs.

△ Personal computers became both more sophisticated and yet cheap enough to buy for the home.

◁ Defence applications continued to fund research. An engineer tests part of a targeting and fire-control system.

▽ In September 1985, a U.S.-French team located and videotaped the wreck of the *Titanic*, the British luxury liner that sank on its maiden voyage in 1912. The ship, broken in two, was found on the ocean floor about 500 miles south of Newfoundland.

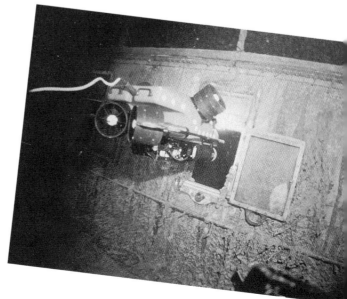

◁ Moment of disaster –
the U.S. space shuttle
Challenger explodes on
takeoff from Cape
Canaveral in January
1986, killling all seven of
its crew.

▷ A view of the planet
Neptune, sent back to
Earth in August 1989 by
space probe *Voyager 2*,
informed scientists of this
unknown planet.

AIDS

HOW BIG DOES IT HAVE TO GET BEFORE YOU TAKE NOTICE?

GAY OR STRAIGHT, MALE OR FEMALE, ANYONE CAN GET AIDS FROM SEXUAL INTERCOURSE. SO THE MORE PARTNERS, THE GREATER THE RISK. PROTECT YOURSELF, USE A CONDOM.

◁ AIDS – Acquired
Immune Deficiency
Syndrome – represented a
challenge both to medical
practice and the public
understanding of the
disease. As the decade
closed, research could offer
no more than hopeful
leads in the search for a
vaccine.

The Enterprise Culture

Encouraged by Ronald Reagan's economic policies, the business community experienced a surge of mergers and corporate takeovers, often financed by "junk" bonds. Defying this trend, American Telephone and Telegraph was divided into many smaller companies.

The success of entrepreneurs like Ted Turner and Donald Trump led students to flock to colleges and universities offering business studies. Others watched television series with corporate settings, such as *Dynasty*, acquired shares, and saw their new wealth threatened by the worldwide stock market crash of October 1987.

As the number of two-income families increased, retail patterns changed. Department store sales declined as shoppers turned to malls, outlets, and discount houses. Specialty mail-order catalogs and television sales channels also became increasingly more popular. However, the successful penetration of American markets by foreign companies and products continued to contribute to the soaring U.S. trade deficit.

△ Rupert Murdoch, Australian-born, American-naturalized publisher who established a worldwide empire in communications, based on publicity stunts, confrontations, and the ruthless application of the latest printing techniques.

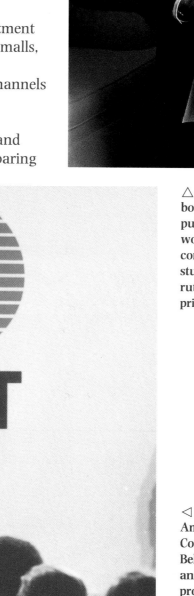

◁ On January 8 1982, the American Telephone and Telegraph Company agreed to divest itself of 22 Bell operating companies to settle an antitrust suit. The new "Baby Bells" prospered, and AT&T began to compete with other long-distance phone companies.

◁ Ted Turner built a television empire which includes network stations and a 24-hour cable news service. He bought up the MGM film library and stirred controversy by "colorizing" black-and-white movies.

◁ In 1989, B. Altman and Company went bankrupt after 75 years in business. Burdened by debts, the department store failed to keep pace with changing retail trends.

△ Tycoon Donald Trump made his fortune in real estate with many Atlantic City hotels and casinos to his name as well as Manhattan commercial and residential buildings. He also owns a shuttle airline.

Sports

During the 1980s, political and financial disputes spilled over into the sports world. Protesting the invasion of Afghanistan, the United States boycotted the 1980 Moscow Olympics, and in response, the Soviet Union refused to attend the 1984 games in Los Angeles. In 1981, a major league baseball strike shut down the ball parks for 50 days, canceling 714 games. When the National Football League players went out on strike in 1982, half the season's games were called off.

The old pattern of Anglo-American dominance disappeared as the Latin countries gained control of international sporting organizations and the enthusiasm for competitive sports spread to produce a cosmopolitan collection of world-class sporting heroes – the Spanish golfer Seve Ballesteros, the Canadian hockey-player Wayne Gretzky, Moroccan middle-distance runner Said Aouita. and the Brazilian racing driver Ayrton Senna. Money and fame provided temptations as well as rewards. Sprinter Carl Lewis set himself self-consciously to be a role model for black youth. Sprinter Ben Johnson, however, admitted that his Olympic success in 1988 was won with the aid of drugs.

△ On September 24, 1988, West-Indian born Ben Johnson won an Olympic gold medal for Canada, setting a new world record for the 100 meters. Within days, he was stripped of his award, having failed a drug test. He later admitted taking steroids over a long period of time.

◁ In 1988, U.S. champion Debi Thomas became the first African-American figure skater to compete in the Olympics. She won a bronze medal at the winter games in Calgary while East German Katarina Witt took the gold.

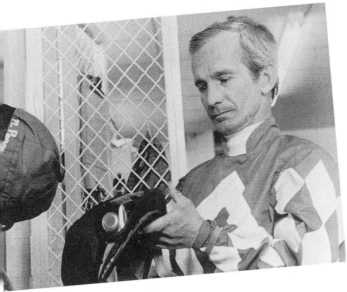

(Above right) America's Florence Griffith-Joyner proved that sports and style could go together, setting new world athletic records for the women's 100 and 200 meters in 1988.

(Top) In 1989, veteran jockey Willie Shoemaker began his final racing tour, with farewell appearances in 20 countries. He has won more races than any other jockey, riding horses in nearly 9,000 competitions.

△ The presence of rock star Sting at a run in aid of famine relief in the Third World showed how the worlds of music and sports shared a concern to use their popular appeal for the benefit of others.

▷ In the 1980s, the English-speaking world's lead in world-class golf was challenged by newcomers like Spain's Seve Ballesteros.

Film

Movies continued their revival in the 1980s, aided rather than undermined by the spread of videotape ownership, which enabled millions to replay "classic" movies in their own homes, reinforcing the status of film as the 20th century mass art form. Film-maker Stephen Spielberg created a string of smash hits with fast-pace fantasy themes to appeal to a broad range of ages and types – *ET*, *Ghostbusters*, *Close Encounters of the Third Kind*, and three starring Harrison Ford, veteran of the successful *Star Wars* series, as Indiana Jones.

The tendency to try to turn a success into a formula was marked. Sylvester Stallone's *Rocky* and *Rambo*, like *Superman*, produced sequels unimaginatively entitled II, III and IV. Britain took Hollywood by storm with the unexpected *Chariots of Fire* and the block-busting *Gandhi*. Australian Paul Hogan's *Crocodile Dundee* proved that a low budget need be no barrier to success, while the mega-flop *Raise the Titanic* proved that a massive budget was no guarantee either.

◁ In 1982, Ben Kingsley won an Oscar for Best Actor for *Gandhi*, which also won Best Film and Best Director. This triple feat was also achieved by *Kramer v. Kramer* (1979), *Amadeus* (1984) and *Rain Man* (1988).

△ In the 1989 version of *Batman*, the publicity preceding its release threatened to overwhelm the film itself.

▽ Paul Hogan's *Crocodile Dundee* reached wider audiences when it was released on video.

◁ The 1989 low-budget, star-studded remake of Shakespeare's *Henry V* was a triumph for its youthful star and director, Kenneth Branagh, showing that Olivier's 1944 version <u>could</u> be bettered.

▷ In *Who Framed Roger Rabbit?*, British character actor Bob Hoskins faced up to a novel professional challenge – acting opposite cartoon characters.

▽ Stephen Spielberg's *Indiana Jones* films combined the appeal of exotic locations and thrilling action sequences while his science fiction fantasy, *ET* (below right), skillfully blended the emotions of laughter and sympathy to produce a film for the whole family.

Music and Musicals

The decade began with a dramatic reminder of the shadow of the 1960s with the murder in New York of ex-Beatle John Lennon. Nineteen-sixties revivals and remakes enjoyed continuing popularity, as did ageing superstars like Stevie Wonder, Tina Turner, Elton John, Cliff Richard, and Paul McCartney.

The decade did, however produce its own big names, such as Bruce Springsteen, Prince, and Whitney Houston. Many broke from groups or duos to become stars in their own right – Diana Ross (ex-Supremes), Sting (ex-Police), George Michael (ex-Wham!) and Phil Collins (ex-Genesis). Among the various bands, Dire Straits and the Irish group U2 proved to be outstanding.

Bob Geldof mobilized fellow musicians to use their fame and talent for the benefit of the world's poor, while Paul Simon's *Graceland* LP used African rhythms to combat apartheid.

◁ In 1983, *A Chorus Line* became the longest running Broadway musical. Performances continued throughout the decade.

▽ The compact disk (CD) brought listeners an unprecedented quality of sound reproduction.

△ The 1980s saw a major revival of the large scale stage musical, especially in Britain. Classically-trained composer Andrew Lloyd-Webber enjoyed enormous success with *Cats, Phantom of the Opera, Starlight Express*, and *Aspects of Love*.

◁ The 1985 Live-Aid Concert for Africa linked Philadelphia and London (left) to raise $70,000,000 for famine relief. Organized by Irish rock musician Bob Geldof it was broadcast to 1,500,000,000 people in 152 countries by the largest international satellite link-up ever. Phil Collins managed to perform live on both sides of the Atlantic at this event.

▽ Dancer, turned drummer/ vocalist, Madonna, sprang to superstardom with three feature films and over a dozen million-seller records in the space of just four years. Her views and style made news on and off the stage.

◁ Michael Jackson beat all previous records when his 1982 album, *Thriller*, sold 37 million copies. The 1987 follow-up, *Bad*, was also a massive commercial hit. Jackson's mastery of showbiz glitz and stagecraft made his 1988 world tour a sell-out before it even started, while his self-obsessed personality and eccentric lifestyle made a best seller out of the autobiographical *Moonwalk*.

Lifestyles

The 1980s was the decade of the "yuppie." Once a term of social analysis (Young Urban Professional), the word passed into common usage and sharpened its meaning to imply upward mobility, greed and aggression. Acutely conscious of lifestyle and image, the classic "yuppie" spent lavishly on brash, designer clothes, ate sparse but expensive "nouvelle cuisine," drove a high-tech car and was seldom more than a few feet away from a portable telephone.

The other major consumer trend was anything but urban. Growing environmental awareness induced manufacturers to reduce the number of aerosol products containing CFCs (chlorofluorocarbons) in favor of "ozone friendly" alternatives and to create "green detergents" and biodegradable packaging. "Greens" and "yuppies" alike shared a common passion for personal health which was reflected in an avoidance of food additives, a preference for organic produce, natural grains and mineral water, a dislike of smoking, and dedication to exercise.

△ A "yuppie" in despair on Black Monday (October 19, 1987) when stock prices crashed worldwide. Note the portable phone and boldly striped shirt – labels of the "breed."

◁ The satellite dish, another electronic addition to houses which had already absorbed the video recorder, calculator, Walkman, and microwave ovens.

▽ Portable telephones, like fax machines, released workers from the need to stay in one place.

△ The compact disk – a new technology which made the old instantly redundant.

▽ Stretch limousines became an important status symbol for the wealthy during the 1980s.

The BODY SHOP
Skin & Hair Care Preparations

△ The Body Shop product range combined health and environmental appeal with attractive packaging.

Fashion and Design

"Vorsprung durch Technik," "Better by Design" – the decade was rich in slogans exploiting the growing awareness that design – the tasteful combination of science and art – not only made products more pleasing to the eye, they also made them sell better. Italy and Japan clearly owed as much of their economic success to design flair as to production techniques.

One leader of the cult was Terence (later Sir Terence) Conran, whose chain stores in the U.S. and Britain offered customers inexpensive yet stylish housewares. He recycled millions of his profits to establish London's first Design Museum and had the pleasure of seeing his son, Jasper, become a name designer in his own right. It was the ultimate glamour career and made Ralph Lauren, Calvin Klein, and Anne Klein not only household names but very wealthy as well.

In Britain, schools added design to the curriculum and politicians urged businessmen to improve product design in the interests of national economic competitiveness. No material artifact, from underwear to skyscrapers, seemed exempt from critical appraisal.

▽ Laura Ashley's fashion empire spread from Britain to Europe, the United States, and Japan, promoting a soft "natural" look in everything from garments to furnishings.

△ Princess Diana's tall, slim figure and mass-media exposure did wonders for Britain's international fashion reputation.

◁ Japanese designer Issey Miyake represented the new challenge from the East to the traditional dominance of Paris – but he did establish his reputation by exhibiting his clothes there.

▽ In 1981, Maya Yang Lin's controversial design for the Vietnam War Memorial (two granite walls inscribed with the names of U.S. war dead) won a nationwide competition.

△ Product designers produced individual juice boxes with built-in straws and squeezable bottles of ketchup and mustard.

Victims

While revolutionary new applications of microchips and lasers brought breathtaking advances in technology and medicine which seemed to confirm human mastery of the material world, the decade also produced dramatic confirmation of its limitations.

Armed conflicts swelled the world's refugee population, especially in Africa, Southeast Asia, and the Middle East. AIDS, a disease which seemed to be beyond the control of modern medical knowledge, plagued both the developed and the developing world. Spectacular natural disasters during the decade included devastating floods in the Sudan and Bangladesh, drought in the Horn of Africa and the explosion of Mount St. Helens as well as the earthquake in San Francisco in the United States and also in Armenia.

Simple human error also played its part. A faulty design led to the collapse of two aerial walkways in a Kansas City hotel, killing 110 people and injuring 190. In Prince William Sound, Alaska, the third mate piloted the oil tanker *Exxon Valdez* into a reef, causing the largest oil spill in U.S. history.

△ Terry Waite, special envoy of the Archbishop of Canterbury, disappeared in Beirut in 1987 while trying to free hostages.

(Left and below) Soccer disasters included the 1985 Bradford City fire, the rampage by Liverpool fans at Brussels' Heysel stadium, and the crushing to death of 95 people at a soccer match in Sheffield, England, in 1989.

◁ An explosion on the North Sea oil rig *Piper Alpha* in 1988 claimed 167 lives – a savage reminder of the perils of operating in a harsh and unpredictable environment.

▽ When Pan Am flight 103 exploded over Lockerbie in Scotland in 1988, 270 lives were lost. A year later, the bomber had still not been traced.

◁ The death from AIDS of film star Rock Hudson (seen here with long-time co-star Doris Day) drew dramatic attention to this frightening disease.

Record Breakers

Each year brought with it a record of some kind. In 1980, Sweden's Bjorn Borg won the men's singles at Wimbledon for the fifth successive time, an unprecedented achievement. In 1989, Texas Ranger Nolan Ryan became the first pitcher in major league baseball history to strike out 5,000 batters during his career.

In 1981, Sandra Day O'Connor became the first woman appointed to the U.S. Supreme Court. In 1982, Korean Reverend Moon married 4,000 couples in a single ceremony in New York. Nineteen eighty-three saw the Australian businessman, Alan Bond, win yachting's prestigious America's Cup from the United States (which it had held for 132 years). In 1984, Mrs. Geraldine Ferraro broke the gender barrier by running for office of U.S. vice-president. The 1985 Live Aid concert was watched by the world's largest-ever television audience. Nineteen eighty-six saw the world's worst-ever nuclear accident at Chernobyl, and in 1987, Margaret Thatcher became the first British prime minister ever to win three general elections in a row. In 1988, Benazir Bhutto became the Muslim world's first woman leader.

△ Martina Navratilova, of the United States, won the women's singles at Wimbledon every year from 1982 to 1987. She had also won the title in 1976 and 1979 playing as a Czech and therefore surpassed Billie Jean King's previous record of six victories.

◁ In July 1981, a solar-powered plane, *Solar Challenger*, piloted by Stephen Ptacek of Golden, Colorado, flew for 5 hours and 22 minutes from Cormeilles-en-Vexin in France to the Royal Air Force base at Manston in Kent to become the first solar-powered aircraft ever to cross the English Channel.

▷ The sale of Van Gogh's *Sunflowers* for £24,750,000 in March 1987 tripled the previous auction price record for a work of art. At the year's end, the same artist's *Irises* set a new record of $53,900,000.

▽ Saturn and its rings, as photographed by NASA's *Voyager 2* in July 1981 when it was still 27,000,000 miles from the planet. In 1989, it sent back thrilling new pictures of Neptune.

▽ The plight of two whales trapped in Arctic ice in 1988 captured worldwide attention and triggered a multinational rescue effort, which did set one of them free.

Personalities of the 1980s

Botha, Pieter Willem (1916-   ), rose through South Africa's dominant Nationalist party to become prime minister in 1978 and state president in 1984. His cautious attempts to reform apartheid were hampered by his wish to be seen as a strong man, resistant to pressure. He was forced from power in 1989 after losing the confidence of Cabinet colleagues.

Ceaucescu, Nicolae (1918–89), son of a peasant and life-long Communist who became party leader in 1965 and president of Rumania in 1974. He combined an independent foreign policy with repressive internal rule and a grotesque cult of personality. His policies impoverished, polluted, and terrorized his country. In December 1989, he was overthrown by a popular rising and shot with his powerful wife, Elina.

Deng Xiao ping (1904–   ), veteran of the Communist struggle for power in China and master of political survival who emerged in 1978 as the single most powerful party official. His liberalization of the economy stimulated prosperity but his "opening to the West" also provoked demands for greater democracy, which led to the Tiananmen Square massacre of 1989. He resigned his last official post later that same year.

Galtieri, Leopoldo Fortunato (1927–   ), Argentine general and president (1981–2) who initiated the forcible seizure of the British-occupied Falkland Islands. Their recapture forced his loss of office and later imprisonment.

Gorbachev, Mikhail (1931–   ), Secretary-general of the Communist Party of the Soviet Union (1985) and president (1988), he committed himself to the rebirth of the Soviet economy through the building of a more open and flexible political system and the reduction of defense spending. His acceptance of nationalist aspirations within the Soviet Union and in Eastern Europe appeared to some to threaten the stability of the entire Soviet system. Others hailed him as the most courageous and imaginative leader of the decade.

Havel, Vaclav (1936–   ), Czech playwright and political activist. Repeatedly imprisoned for his criticisms of the Communist regime, he emerged as a key figure in the popular uprising which led to its fall in 1989.

Kohl, Helmut (1930–   ), veteran Christian Democrat who led the West German parliamentary opposition from 1976 and succeeded as chancellor of the Federal Republic of Germany in 1982. Reputedly dull, he showed a skillful mixture of vision and caution when suddenly confronted with the possibility of German reunification in 1989.

Marcos, Ferdinand Edralin (1917–89   , traded on a largely spurious reputation as a wartime resistance leader to become president of the Philippines in 1965. His anti-communist gestures won American support, but his increasingly corrupt and dictatorial rule led to his overthrow in 1986. In exile he resisted attempts to recover the vast fortune he had acquired while in office.

Mitterand, François Maurice (1916–   ), resistance fighter turned politician, he became the first socialist president of the French Fifth Republic in 1981 and was re-elected in 1988. A firebrand in his youth, he represented in old age the type of the French gentleman.

Mugabe, Robert Gabriel (1925–   ), founder of the Zimbabwe African National Union (ZANU) in 1963. imprisoned by the white-dominated Rhodesian regime (1964–74), became co-leader of the Patriotic Front in 1976 and coordinator of the guerilla independence movement. A self-styled Marxist, he became prime minister in 1980 and showed himself moderate in everything except his determination to hold onto power.

Palme, Olaf (1927–86), Social Democratic prime minister of Sweden from 1969–76 and 1982–86. He kept his country out of the EEC, criticized U.S. policy in

Pieter Willem Botha

Mikhail Gorbachev

Helmut Kohl

Vietnam and promoted Third World development. He was deeply mourned after his apparently motiveless murder in a Stockholm street. Long, controversial police inquiries led to the arrest and conviction of a suspect who was subsequently freed.

Reagan, Ronald (1911–   ), radio sports commentator and movie star, the "great communicator" came to politics as a union negotiator for actors. Serving his apprenticeship as governor of California (1967–74), he became America's president in 1980 and won a second term by a landslide in 1984. He was indifferent to detail and open to charges of laziness and over-reliance on subordinates whose standards of loyalty and honor sometimes fell far short of his own. Americans loved him for restoring their self-confidence, but critics accused him of failing to tackle the country's fundamental weaknesses in runaway public expenditure and declining economic performance.

Sadat, Anwar al- (1918–81), a close supporter of Nasser in the Free Officers movement which overthrew King Farouk in 1952. He served as vice-president of Egypt twice before succeeding Nasser as president in 1970. His 1973 war with Israel was inconclusive, but his 1977 visit to the Israeli Knesset led to a peace settlement and a sharing of the 1978

Nobel Peace Prize with Israeli Prime Minister Menachem Begin. This cost Egypt the hostility of the Arab world and Sadat his life at the hands of Muslim extremists.

Sakharov, Andrei (1921–89), a brilliant nuclear scientist who worked to develop the Soviet Union's bomb but forfeited his privileged position by denouncing the arms race and dictatorial rule. In 1975, he became the first Soviet citizen to win the Nobel Peace Prize. Sentenced to internal exile in 1980 and released in 1987, he became a leading opposition member in the Congress of the People's Deputies. An unflinching campaigner for human rights, he was recognized as the conscience of the nation and his sudden death from a heart attack was widely mourned at home and abroad.

Thatcher, Margaret Hilda (1925–   ), the Oxford-scholarship girl who qualified as both a chemist and a lawyer before marrying a wealthy businessman. MP for prosperous Finchley in 1959, she served as minister of education before replacing Edward Heath as leader of the Conservative Party in 1975 and prime minister in 1979, the first female leader of a Western democracy. An early hardline anti-Soviet stance won her a reputation as "the Iron Lady," which was strengthened by Britain's victory

in the Falkland Islands. Hardworking, bossy, and impatient of opposition, she had, by 1988, served longer than any prime minister since Asquith.

Tito, Josip Broz (1892–1980), head of the Yugoslav Communist Party from 1937 and leader of anti-fascist partisan resistance. He created postwar Yugoslavia and, through his independent foreign policy, developed a "nonaligned" movement for nations eager to escape super-power influences. His death exposed his country's economic decline and ethnic disunity.

Walesa, Lech (1943–   ), a Gdansk shipyard electrician, he became Solidarity's leader in 1980. He was interned under martial law (1981–2) and awarded the Nobel Peace Prize in 1983. Dogged in pursuit of freedom, he avoided extremism and in 1989 saw a non-Communist government installed, but refused to lead it himself although he was seen to be Poland personified.

Yamani, Sheikh Ahmed Zaki (1930–   ), the master tactician of Saudi oil policy (1962–86), he engineered the 1970s oil price rise while diplomatically keeping the OPEC cartel intact until his sudden fall from power.

François Mitterand

Robert Mugabe

Andrei Sakharov

1980s year by year

1980

- Protesting the invasion of Afghanistan, the U.S. suspends grain sales to the Soviet Union.
- Gdansk shipyard strike leads to birth of Solidarity, the Polish trade union.
- Robert Mugabe becomes Prime Minister of an independent Zimbabwe.
- Failure of the United States' attempt to rescue Iran hostages
- Iraqi attack on Iran starts Gulf War.
- Reagan wins U.S. presidential election.
- Mrs. Gandhi reelected in India.
- Mount St. Helens erupts in the state of Washington.
- Beatle John Lennon shot dead.
- General Motors introduce first "seeing" robot.

1981

- Marriage of Prince Charles and Lady Diana Spencer.
- Assassination attempts on the Pope and President Reagan.
- Sandra Day O'Connor becomes first woman appointed to the U.S. Supreme Court.
- Two aerial walkways collapse in Kansas City hotel, killing 110 people.
- Release of American Embassy hostages in Iran.
- Israel bombs Iraqi nuclear reactor.
- First reports of AIDS received.
- First heart-lung transplant.
- First compact disks on sale.
- *Columbia*, the world's first reusable spacecraft, successfully launched from Cape Canaveral.

1982

- American Telephone and Telegraph agrees to be divided into smaller companies.
- Israeli forces invade Lebanon.
- Lebanese President Gemayel killed.
- Christian militias massacre Palestinian refugees in Beirut.
- *U.S.A. Today* begins publication.
- Cyanide placed in Tylenol capsules causes the death of seven people in Chicago.
- National Football league players' strike results in cancellation of half the season's games.
- Astronomers report first sighting of Halley's Comet.
- Greenham Common Peace Camp set up to protest against installation of United States Cruise missiles on British soil.
- The Equal Rights Amendment fails to win ratification.
- First pocket-sized television set introduced.
- First artificial heart transplant operation is completed.

1983

- Harold Washington elected first black mayor of Chicago.
- Sally Ride becomes first American woman astronaut in space.
- IRA bomb planted outside Harrods.
- Americans celebrate 100th anniversary of the Brooklyn Bridge.
- Vatican art collection tours major cities in the United States.
- Suicide bombers kill 241 American Marines and 58 French paratroopers in Lebanon.
- PLO withdraws from Lebanon to Tunisia.
- President Reagan announces "Star Wars" program – Strategic Defense Initiative (SDI).
- Federal Trade Commission approves joint Japanese-American

auto venture.
- First World Athletics Championships.
- Derby-winning racehorse Shergar kidnapped.
- U.S. troops invade Grenada.
- President Alfonsin restores democratic rule in Argentina.
- Russian fighters shoot down a South Korean 747 airliner in Soviet airspace, killing 269.

1984

- Mrs. Gandhi assassinated and succeeded by son Rajiv as prime minister of India.
- Bhopal chemical disaster kills 2,000 people and maims 200,000 others.
- Extensive fighting in Beirut.
- Chernenko succeeds Andropov in the Soviet Union.
- President Reagan reelected for a second term of office.
- Bell laboratories announces development of the megabit computer memory chip.
- IRA bombs Grand Hotel in Brighton during Conservative Party conference, killing four.
- Russia boycotts Los Angeles' Olympics.
- Band Aid appeal for relief of famine in Ethiopia.
- United States withdraws from UNESCO.

1985

- Liverpool fans rampage at Heysel Stadium in Brussels killing 41 Italian and Belgian supporters.
- Terry Waite, envoy of the Archbishop of Canterbury, negotiates the freedom of four British hostages in Beirut.
- Israelis bomb PLO offices in Tunis.
- Palestinian guerillas attempt to hijack Italian cruise liner.

- South Africa ends ban on mixed marriages but declares state of emergency.
- French-American team discovers wreckage of the *Titanic* on ocean floor.
- Hurricane Gloria wreaks havoc on the East Coast of the United States.
- Earthquake damages Mexico City.
- Major famine in Ethiopia.
- Greenpeace ship *Rainbow Warrior* sunk by French secret service.
- Death of Enver Hoxha, Albania's Communist dictator for over 40 years.
- Mikhail Gorbachev comes to power in the Soviet Union.

1986

- American space shuttle *Challenger* self-destructs on takeoff.
- Chernobyl nuclear reactor meltdown.
- United States bombs Libya.
- "Irangate" scandal.
- Corazon Aquino ousts Ferdinand Marcos in the Philippines.
- "Baby Doc" Duvalier loses power in Haiti.
- Esso and Barclays Bank withdraw investments from South Africa.
- Robert Penn Warren becomes first official United States Poet Laureate.
- Liberty weekend celebrates restoration of the Statue of Liberty.
- Prince Andrew marries Sarah Ferguson.

1987

- Mrs. Thatcher wins third election.
- Brazil suspends payment on debts owed to international commercial banks.
- Pope visits Latin America.
- Terry Waite taken hostage.
- Austrian president Kurt Waldheim barred from entering the United States.
- West German teenager Mathias

Rost lands light plane in Red Square and is arrested.
- United States celebrates bicentennial of the constitution.
- International treaty signed to protect ozone layer in the atmosphere.
- "Black Monday" sees stock markets collapse worldwide.
- Army coup in Fiji declares it a republic and withdraws it from the Commonwealth.
- Gorbachev begins reforms in the Soviet Union.
- Reagan and Gorbachev agree to begin nuclear disarmament at Washington summit.

1988

- The Soviet Union withdraws troops from Afghanistan.
- American warship shoots down Iranian airbus killing 290 passengers.
- Ceasefire ends Iran/Iraq war.
- Olympic Games held in Seoul.
- Earthquake devastates Soviet Armenia.
- President Zia of Pakistan killed in plane crash.
- Referendum ends General Pinochet's rule in Chile.
- George Bush defeats Michael Dukakis to win the U.S. presidential election.
- American courts indict Panamanian leader General Noriega on drugs charges.
- U.S. space shuttle program recommences.
- Yasser Arafat addresses the United Nations and enters discussions with the United States.
- Fire devastates 1.1 million acres in Yellowstone National Park.
- Pan Am flight 103 explodes over Lockerbie, Scotland, killing 300 people.
- North Sea oil rig *Piper Alpha* explodes, killing 166.

1989

- Gorbachev visits Beijing.
- Chinese army massacres 1,000 protesters in Tiananmen Square.
- Death of Emperor Hirohito in Japan.
- Muslims protest against the publication of Salman Rushdie's book, *The Satanic Verses.*
- Hurricane Hugo sweeps through the Caribbean, resulting in immense property damage and more than 50 deaths.
- Death of Ayatollah Khomeini.
- United Nations organizes World Environment Day.
- Earthquake devastates San Francisco.
- Tanker hits reef in Alaskan waters, causing largest oil spill in U.S. history.
- Rajiv Gandhi loses Indian general election.
- Pakistan rejoins the Commonwealth.
- American invasion of Panama forces General Noriega to face up to drugs charges.
- Fall of Communist governments in Poland, East Germany, Hungary, Czechoslovakia, Bulgaria, and Rumania.

Index

PRINTED IN BELGIUM BY